C000108571

# RELEASING ENERGY

GS Misc 599

# RELEASING ENERGY

## How Methodists and Anglicans Can Grow Together

**Flora Winfield**

CHURCH HOUSE
PUBLISHING

Church House Publishing
Church House
Smith Street
London
SW1P 3NZ

ISBN 0 7151 5760 4

Published 2000 for the Council for Christian Unity of the Church of England by Church House Publishing.

*Copyright © The Archbishops' Council 2000*

All rights reserved. Churches and Church organizations have permission to reproduce this publication in part or in its entirety for local use, provided the copies include the above copyright notice and no charge is made for them. Any other reproduction, storage or transmission of material from this publication by any means or in any form, electronic or mechanical, including photocopying, recording, or any information storage and retrieval system, requires written permission which should be sought from the Copyright and Contracts Administrator, The Archbishops' Council, Church of England, Church House, Great Smith Street, London SW1P 3NZ (Tel: 020 7898 1557; Fax: 020 7898 1449; Email: copyright@c-of-e.org.uk).

*This report has only the authority of the Council which produced it.*

Printed in England by Halstan & Co. Ltd

# Contents

# Introduction

A survey of ecumenical life in England would result in a map showing plenty of uneven ground. In some places, long-established relations between Christians of different denominations have borne fruit in mature, committed ecumenical sharing: this is the hill country. In others, we have yet to meet one another: these are the plains. In some places, ecumenical officers struggle to keep the topography above sea level; in others, ecumenical living and working is an accepted natural way of being and becoming the Church together.

The relations between Methodists and Anglicans in England share this characteristic unevenness, as they relate to one another and to other partner churches. The reasons for the hills and plains are manifold: geography, the distribution of Methodists and Anglicans, the theological approaches of those in positions of influence both now and in the past, the history of an area, the personalities involved. There are places where Methodists and Anglicans live and worship alongside one another, and yet have barely encountered one another, and there are many places where Methodists and Anglicans live and worship in close relationship with one another and with partners from other churches, so that it is hard, and perhaps rather artificial, to describe this relationship in isolation from our other partnerships.

Another difficulty in preparing this book has been that in many situations people, including church leaders, are reluctant to talk publicly about their experience of growing together – either because they fear that some person in authority will tell them what they are doing is 'not allowed', or because they feel that relations are still fragile and may be damaged by exposure.

## Releasing Energy: How Methodists and Anglicans can grow together

This publication is aimed primarily at parish clergy and circuit ministers, readers and local preachers and other interested lay people. It is designed to reach parts of the Church of England and the Methodist Church not previously inspired by the ecumenical vision, as well as those where there is already a commitment to working together.

*Releasing Energy* is designed to stimulate and encourage developing relationships between local churches, deaneries and circuits, dioceses and districts. Its focus is practical, and aims to provide examples of good practice and pilot projects from a variety of areas: it is not comprehensive – there are lots of other good examples – but is intended to help both Churches to think creatively.

The book has been produced to support and underpin the work of growth in fellowship, witness and common life which is vital to the progress of the Formal Conversations between the Church of England and the Methodist Church, currently in progress and which began in 1999. Its production was endorsed by the Formal Conversations teams at their meeting in October 1999.

## What is the agenda for releasing energy?

This agenda, shaped by the work of the preliminary talks between the Church of England and the Methodist Church, calls both Churches to take seriously the possibilities for their growth in fellowship together, during the time of the Formal Conversations. The agenda is very wide ranging, and touches the lives of both Churches at every level, calling us to growth in fellowship in:

1. the sharing of worship;

2. prayer for and with each other and the building up of a common life in mission and service;

3. the extension of Local Ecumenical Partnerships (LEPs) wherever Methodists and Anglicans live and worship in the same locality;

4. the rationalization of the use of buildings wherever Anglicans and Methodists live in close proximity;

5. closer cooperation in deaneries and circuits, together with the rationalization of ecclesiastical boundaries to serve the mission of the Church;

6. more effective deployment of ministers, especially in rural areas and urban priority areas;

7. the exchange of experience of women's ministry and of the experience of living with two recognized positions on the ordination of women to the presbyterate;

8.  joint processes of selection for ministry;

9.  increased provision for joint theological education for both lay and ordained;

10. joint decisions over who may be ordained, the appointment or stationing of ministers, matters of church property, etc.

- What might a ten-point agenda for growing into unity include in your locality?

## Is it our agenda?

There are many areas of our lives as churches where we already live and work closely together: in Local Ecumenical Partnerships, in projects for mission and service in local communities, in work with children and young people. In most of these, the relationship between the Church of England and the Methodist Church is set within the context of a network of partnerships with other churches, which remain important to us. However, during the period of the Formal Conversations, we should seek to deepen our understanding of one another's traditions in every area of our lives, so that we grow more closely together as churches, into that living temple which God calls us to become. In this process, we need to be able to listen to one another's traditions in new ways – to be able to receive from one another those gifts, visions and insights which are lost to us as a result of our division. This time of special concentration on our partnership as churches requires a firm commitment and leadership from those who exercise responsibility in our churches. A vision for the possible needs to replace the sense of defeat we sometimes feel about what is too difficult. Our shared calling to mission and service to a broken and divided world is too important for us to allow it to be impeded by our broken and divided churches.

## So what is asked of us?

For the Formal Conversations to bear fruit, it is vital that each Methodist and Church of England congregation, circuit, deanery, diocese and district participates in the process. These conversations are not only the responsibility of those appointed by the Churches to represent them at the meetings, but of those at every level of each Church's life, and we will need to be open to being renewed together, living with:

- an expectation that our partnership is a place where the Holy Spirit is at work, and therefore...

- a willingness to be changed by our experience of partnership: ecumenism is transformatory, and growing together as churches will release energy for mission.

- a lively vision that we are more than the sum of our parts, and that in growing together we are not watering down our traditions, but rather enriching them;

- a creativity, in response to mission opportunities, developing our traditions, structures and ministries together;

- a recognition that we have much to learn from one another, that each of us has that which the other lacks;

- a spirit of listening to the ways in which God is already at work in our experience of being the church together. This agenda for growing together and releasing energy does not run parallel to the Formal Conversations; it is an integral part of their work, as they receive insights and possibilities from the lives of the churches and test their theological progress within this context of developing relationships.

In all this, the role of leaders in both Churches is vital: there is enthusiasm and creativity at the grass roots in both our Churches, but people need to be encouraged and to feel that they have permission to go on growing in partnership together and to try out new ideas and ways of working.

## Is it worth the effort?

Most of all, the powerful gospel imperative for the Churches' renewed concentration on our relationship needs to be expressed in a lively and compelling way. Otherwise, there is always the danger that the time of conversation appears to be about two Churches talking about churchy things. Few people can find the energy to face the hard issues of Christian disunity unless they find our divisions offensive, and unless they also hold on to a vision of our unity where the Holy Spirit is at work.

The situations described in the following pages offer some practical examples for releasing energy and growing together.

# Growing Together in Rural Areas

## In village communities

❖    In the **Diocese of Gloucester** and the **Bristol District** the village of **Leonard Stanley** is an example of fruit borne of a long-standing relationship, as churches have grown together. For many years the congregations of the parish church and chapel have lived and worked together in ministry to the whole village community. When the chapel building became unsafe, the Anglicans invited the Methodists to come and share the parish church as a new united congregation, bringing with them those elements of their Methodist inheritance which seemed most precious. On Easter Day morning in 1993, the Methodists met for worship in the chapel for the last time, and gathering up things which represented the treasures of their tradition, they processed across the green to the parish church carrying Bibles, hymn-books, trays of communion cups, the Sunday school banner and the cross from the communion table. They were welcomed into the parish church to join the celebration of Christ's resurrection. The life of the whole Christian community in the village has been renewed by this coming together, and the parish church building is now also used by the Roman Catholic villagers for a mass each Saturday evening. A member of the congregation remarked on the day that the new joint congregation was inaugurated: 'We are a whole which is much more than the sum of its parts.'

❖    In many rural communities with only one worshipping congregation, the *Declaration of Ecumenical Welcome and Commitment* offers a way of welcoming and affirming the contribution of members of a partner church resident in a village, in the life and worship of the village church, without the formation of a Local Ecumenical Partnership (the Declarations for Anglican or Methodist churches can be found at the end of this book).

## Across wider areas

❖    The Rural Affairs Committees of the Church of England and the Methodist Church now hold a joint meeting each September to share their work.

❖ In North Lincolnshire, in the **Diocese of Lincoln** and the **Lincoln and Grimsby District,** five deaneries and circuits are considering how they can grow together into united Anglican-Methodist areas.

## Case study: North Lincolnshire

The **Yarborough Deanery** and the **Barton and Brigg Circuits** are the areas in which this thinking is furthest advanced.

### THE AIM

Recognizing our legitimate diversity, the aim is to work together to enable and nurture mission and ministry by Anglican and Methodist Church people in Christ's name across the area we jointly serve, sharing vision, concerns and resources.

### THE PROCESS

A joint steering group has been established to:

- collate strategic thinking;

- develop joint decision-making processes;

- coordinate agendas between the three partner bodies;

- foster initiatives to increase local partnership between churches.

Collaboration with Christians of other traditions is invited.

### THE MOTIVATION

People need to see us working together to address the issues that matter to them. We can learn from each other as we pray about and reflect theologically on God's will for this area. We need to make better use of personnel, buildings and our limited resources.

### ACROSS THE AREA THIS COOPERATION IS VISIBLE THROUGH:

- church leaders of the two denominations who pray together regularly;

- closer coordination of agendas between deanery synod and circuit meetings;

- shared priorities and the use of the resources of both traditions;

- new joint initiatives to express the gospel to people in the area;

- shared prayer, study and training.

**MORE LOCALLY WE WORK TOWARDS:**

- a climate which can encourage Christ's disciples in all traditions to think creatively about how their mission can be credible in their locality;

- affirmation and encouragement for existing joint activity.

**FURTHER POSSIBILITIES INCLUDE:**

- shared church government (joint meetings or a joint church council);

- enjoying a shared ministry by ministers from both traditions;

- joint ventures such as children's or youth work or ministry in old people's homes.

## Case study: North Yorkshire

The **Thirsk and Northallerton Circuit** and the **Mowbray Deanery** are more or less coterminus with each other, covering the same geographical area.

There is a Local Ecumenical Partnership at Osmotherley. This comprises a Methodist church, an Anglican parish church and a Roman Catholic church. The local vicar is Recognized and Regarded as a Methodist minister. Although each church holds a separate Sunday service there is considerable sharing during the week. The Methodists and Anglicans hold a service of Holy Communion each Wednesday, alternating between the two buildings.

As a consequence of the LEP all three Methodist ministers in the circuit are members of the Mowbray Deanery chapter meeting. This has allowed a mutual sharing and enabled us to learn from each other and grow together.

A local covenant has been signed by the churches in Northallerton. This has come about by the strengthened Anglican/Methodist relationships and includes the United Reformed Church, Roman Catholic and Baptist Churches.

Recently, an Information Technology Project entitled RITES (Rural IT Education Services) has been established in partnership with Northallerton College which is providing training personnel. This project has been funded by Hambleton District Council and by British Telecom.

The scheme has six lap-top computers and a server. The training is being carried out at Appleton Wiske Methodist Church. This has a membership of ten, and five years ago was extensively refurbished. On Fridays people of all ages come to their local chapel and learn basic IT skills. It is hoped that those who wish to follow this up will use their new-found skills to join a course at the college, use it as a stepping-stone to re-training for work, or use it in the work environment or at home. Those who have tasted and seen are keen and excited by the local project. Other venues are in the pipeline such as other local churches/chapels and halls in other villages. A local garage is sponsoring a car whereby the equipment can be transported from site to site.

The RITES programme has come about because of the ecumenical partnership between the Church of England and the Methodist Church. This ecumenical partnership has drawn them into partnership with the local college and has been resourced by the district council, BT, and a local garage.

## Case study: Melbury

## An Anglican/Methodist Local Ecumenical Partnership in rural West Dorset

### THE AREA

There are 20 villages in the Frome valley off the A37 Dorchester to Yeovil road. This is a farming area and the population of the 19 parishes is less than 4,000. The largest village is Maiden Newton. There are 20 church buildings in the area, including 2 chapels of ease, 3 private chapels and 1 redundant church. All have regular services held in them.

### BACKGROUND

The area has been a Church of England team ministry for many years and there was a Methodist chapel in Maiden Newton. In 1987 an Anglican/Methodist Joint Congregation LEP was established. Worship took place in the parish church and the Methodist chapel was sold.

The Methodist circuit superintendent from Dorchester and other preachers led some services, and a Methodist Communion service was held four times a year. In 1995 the Maiden Newton LEP was reviewed and a point for consideration was the widening of the LEP to include all parishes and the Dorchester Methodist Circuit. This idea was accepted by the Melbury Team Council and the Methodist Circuit.

## THE PROCESS

A draft covenant was produced by the ecumenical officer with the Melbury team ministers and the Methodist circuit superintendent in 1996. It was sent to Churches Together in Dorset, the Salisbury Diocesan Ecumenical Team and the Methodist Faith and Order Committee. Points in the covenant included:

- the extension of the area covered;

- the continuing Methodist services and ministry in Maiden Newton;

- occasional services led by Methodists in other churches in the area covered;

- occasional services led by Anglican members of the team in churches of the Methodist circuit;

- exploration of widening the partnership to include other denominations.

The final form of the covenant and a simple constitution were accepted by the denominations by the end of 1996. The constitution specifically excluded joint confirmations at that time and there was to be no financial transaction involved. The united service to celebrate and sign the covenant was held on 8 April 1997 with the Bishop of Sherborne and the chairman of the Southampton Methodist District.

## THE MELBURY PARTNERSHIP

There are three full-time and one part-time Anglican team vicars for the area. The rector left in January 1998 and has not yet been replaced, so one acts as 'team coordinator'. The area was separated from the Beaminster Deanery and for a few months was a deanery in its own right.

It was then incorporated into the Sherborne Deanery. The Dorchester Methodist Circuit has eight churches, none of which is in the Melbury team area. The superintendent is the only stipendiary minister, with four supernumerary ministers. The circuit covers an area which includes parts of four Anglican benefices other than the Melbury team. The largest church in the circuit is the Dorchester United (Methodist/URC) Church, which is served by two ministers, one from each denomination. The URC minister is a Recognized and Regarded minister of the circuit and participates in the partnership on this basis. Worship includes a Methodist service at Maiden Newton once a month and there is also a Methodist communion service which is held quarterly. Methodist services are held irregularly at other churches in the team area. The Anglican ministers have not yet led services in the Dorchester United Church or other Methodist churches in the circuit. There is a Methodist representative on the Melbury Team Council and an Anglican Melbury team representative on the Dorchester Circuit meeting. There are occasions for informal coming together, such as when the United Church choir participates in the Maiden Newton Flower Festival service, and the Maiden Newton Methodist class meeting has members of several denominations attending. Local church events are supported by members of both denominations and notices of events are given to both.

ISSUES

The boundary issue was handled by taking the already defined Melbury team parishes as the area covered. This means that only a part of the Dorchester Methodist Circuit is inside the geographical area of the partnership. Dorchester itself is specifically outside the area. There is therefore an issue surrounding the leading of services by Anglicans from the Melbury team in the circuit churches. A meeting was held in October 1996 to resolve this and it was agreed that the relevant Anglican incumbents would be notified of intended invitations, by sending them the draft circuit plan. The reorganization of the deaneries means that the Anglicans will relate more to Sherborne than to Dorchester. Informal discussion is in hand with the circuit superintendent of the Sherborne Methodist Circuit. There are a few practicalities to be tackled, such as clarifying the names of contacts for Methodist preachers leading services in the less well-known villages.

THE FUTURE

Relationships are developing positively among the ministers and the representatives on councils. The informal exchanges and sharing in services is beginning to extend the awareness of the partnership to more people in the area, but this cannot be taken for granted.

The deanery reorganization and its implications need care in working through the new structures. The involvement of the URC will be explored when the new minister is appointed at the Dorchester United Church. It is intended that the URC will be specifically included when the constitution is next revised.

The possibilities for Roman Catholic involvement will be explored. The Dorchester Roman Catholic priest favours more house masses in the villages for those who cannot travel in to Dorchester (the nearest parish church). The partnership has developed from a strong sense of what it means to be the Church in each place. It has proceeded in a spirit of openness to possibilities and an acceptance of the mixed denominational backgrounds of those in the village churches. As such it is an interesting model for what is possible in our rural areas, where the only church buildings are Church of England parish churches.

*Mrs Val Potter*
*County Ecumenical Officer for Dorset*

---

If you are in the countryside –

- Is your church the only worshipping congregation in the village? If so, you could think about making the *Declaration of Ecumenical Welcome and Commitment*.

- What about your partner deanery or circuit? How could you work together more closely to serve your communities' needs, as well as working at sharing ministries and worshipping together.

- Do the churches in your area share the task of Agricultural or Rural Chaplaincy?

# Growing Together in Urban Areas

## Case study: Swindon

Parks and Walcot is a post-war estate on the eastern side of the town, with a population of 13,500. It began as a London overspill, and almost all of the housing is council although some properties have now been sold on. In a borough with almost full employment, employment on the estate, especially amongst young people, remains high. The estate suffers by reputation, and often in real terms, from a high incidence of criminality, drug abuse, and neighbour nuisance. On the other hand, there is a large number of community initiatives, and the church has been particularly involved in 'drop in' centres, a credit union, and work with the families of drug users. There are four main churches: a Church of England parish church adjacent to the central shopping area, a Methodist church serving the estate and also an area of more prosperous housing to the west, a Church of England 'daughter church' in the northern part of the estate where there are fewer community facilities but the deprivation factors are larger, and a Roman Catholic church serving both this estate and the largely owner-occupied estate to the east. All these churches are in a long-established Local Ecumenical Partnership.

Until recently the Anglican team ministry comprised two priests, a curate, and a full-time lay administrator. There was a resident Methodist minister who also looked after two other churches in the circuit. Two years ago it became clear that the diocesan allocation would need to be reduced for reasons of availability of clergy rather than finance. At the same time the circuit was faced with the need to lose one minister, primarily for financial reasons. Discussions began between the circuit superintendent and the suffragan bishop, who set up a small group which included the local minister, and which will soon become a sub-group of the new Swindon Sponsoring Body. The basic factors were:

- the estate needed ministers who were resident and committed to the community;

- the style of ministry had to be directly related to the need of the estate;

- mission required that resources be pooled wherever possible;

- there were too many church buildings.

On this last point progress has been slow. The original decision to withdraw from the northern part of the estate was overturned because of the distinct identity and the special needs of this area: the church has been demolished, and the hall will be redeveloped for church/community use, with a Church of England/Methodist Sharing Agreement, and weekday use by a borough-funded Family Centre. Decisions about the parish church and the Methodist church are more difficult: the first is in the right location, the other is a better building and has a stronger congregation. Through all of this the Anglican and Methodist congregations are growing together and worshipping together more. Roman Catholic participation is supportive but unlikely to result in much joint development. The real breakthrough, and perhaps a pattern which others in the process of growing into unity might like to consider, is in the area of ministry. In addition to what the lay people are doing together, the diocese and the circuit have established a three-person team, using the three 'stipends' from the diocesan funds:

- Anglican vicar;

- Methodist minister;

- Lay minister (an Anglican reader living and working in the northern area).

This means that the Church of England is paying the salary and housing costs of the Methodist minister. His ministry is full-time on the estate, although the membership of his church continues to draw from outside, and he remains a member of the circuit staff with occasional duties elsewhere in the circuit.

The advantages to the Methodist church are:

- maintaining ministerial employment;

- honouring its commitment to Urban Priority Area work;

- freeing circuit funds for other work, in this case securing the full-time Methodist appointment in one of the other Swindon Local Ecumenical Partnerships.

The advantages to the Church of England are:

- maintaining its commitment to three 'stipendiary' posts in this Urban Priority Area;

9

- a financial saving because the payment to the circuit is less than the cost of a full-time Anglican priest;

- saving one clergy post, so allowing another parish to have a priest at a time when the national allocation of clergy to the diocese is being reduced.

*The Rt Revd Michael Doe*
*Bishop of Swindon*

❖   On Merseyside, in the **Liverpool Diocese** and **District,** two new Anglican-Methodist Local Ecumenical Partnerships are being established. The Church of St Francis, at Kew, on a new housing development, has started from scratch and developed the presence of the church in a new area altogether. Nearby, two much longer established congregations are coming together – Wesley, Southbank Road, and SS Philip and Paul have decided to form a united congregation, and have begun worshipping together following a Covenant service. After a period of alternating between the two churches they plan to settle in one building, bringing together the traditions and practices of both churches in worship and mission.

If you are in an urban area –

- How are you responding together to the particular needs of your locality?

- What support can you give to projects of your partner church, to work on your behalf?

- Can you explore together the more flexible deployment of ministers?

- How can you share buildings, people and other resources?

# Growing Together in Ministry

## Case study: The Church of Reconciliation, Scunthorpe

The Church of Reconciliation is situated on the **Westcliff Estate** in Scunthorpe, North Lincolnshire (in the **Diocese of Lincoln** and the **Lincoln and Grimsby District**). Westcliff is an estate largely made up of local authority housing, but with a fringe of private dwellings; the population is 7,500. The area was developed during the late 1970s and as the houses became occupied a group of Christians began to meet for worship in the local pub, 'The Desert Rat'. After they outgrew the room there they moved to the wooden youth centre nearby. It was there that, in cooperation with the Church of England, Methodist and United Reformed Churches, they began to plan to build church premises. This came about, however, only after the possibility of shared accommodation in the community centre failed to work out. The site which had been apportioned for the church was in the centre of the estate, with a room for dual purpose building and a clergy house, which in practice was a vicarage as the Anglican church paid for it to be built. The church itself, a part of the site, was built through money raised by the growing congregation. Members went round selling 'bricks' made of paper. The people used their own skills in the building as far as possible, and eventually, some 16 years ago, the building was opened as a three-way Local Ecumenical Partnership with a resident Anglican living in the vicarage, and input from clergy of the other two denominations. From the Anglican point of view, the Church of Reconciliation, as it was named, was at that time a daughter church of St Hugh, New Brumby and had close links with the clergy team there.

In 1992 it was decided that the ministry of the church in the area would be more visible and more effective if it had one minister, who would be recognized by all three churches as their representative to the people. Through the Sponsoring Body, the bishop and other church leaders agreed that a rotating ministry would take place there, beginning with that of the Methodist Church. The person appointed would be accepted by both the other churches, and would be paid by their own denomination, within the financial arrangements already in place, i.e. that when the minister was a Methodist, the circuit would receive a certain proportion of Anglican money and URC money towards ministry, their proportion of quota sent to the diocese and district being reduced by this amount.

With this as the background I took up post in September 1994: at my recognition service I was welcomed and commissioned by the Chairman of the Methodist district, the Bishop of Lincoln and the Moderator of the East Midlands Province of the URC. Some time later I was presented with a letter giving me the 'cure of souls' for the District of Westcliff within the parish of St Hugh. The reason for this lay not with the Westcliff people but with some members of St Hugh's church who found it hard to cope with a 'Methodist team vicar', and sought clarification of my role.

In practical terms the situation was a very positive one. The people of the estate recognized the one church as their church; there was no choice as to where anyone had their child baptized, Church of Reconciliation (COR) was where they came. The situation for funerals was similar, although not many funerals in Scunthorpe take place within church buildings as the Crematorium chapel and grounds are very beautiful. However, in the four years I worked there, I never heard of any requests for funerals which were not those of regular members of another church, which did not come to me, as their vicar.

Worship at COR took an agreed form, using eucharistic liturgy worked out and approved by the denominations: there were three variations which gave enough scope for the traditions involved. Similarly a baptism liturgy was worked out for use at Westcliff alone. Each week there was a Eucharist at some time on Sunday – on the first, third and fifth (if there was one) this would be the main 10 a.m. service. On the second and fourth Sundays morning worship would be Free Church style, with a Eucharist on the second Sunday in the evening and on the fourth at 8.30 a.m. followed by breakfast. A midweek Eucharist took place at 9.15 a.m. three times a month, and at noon on the fourth Wednesday when it would be followed by a simple lunch in aid of charity.

Within a few months of my arrival all worship became all age; this was because of the nature of the estate. We had very few children coming regularly to the Sunday school, and in common with many churches a shortage of those who felt led to teach them, and who were willing to miss out on worship themselves to do so. On the other hand, sometimes as many as 20 children would turn up off the street, and it was clear that they felt very much at home. Such a situation could be difficult for visiting preachers, but it became well known, and on those occasions when visits by the local preachers or other clergy were planned, they were warned well in advance that they might as easily have no children as 20, so they were well prepared.

In church government, the congregation elected their own church council which was lay-chaired; this was a great release to the minister who attended simply as a member with no particular role. There were on the council nominated representatives of the trustees who were made up of the sponsoring churches. Following the pattern of the Australian United Church, elders were appointed who took on the role of pastoral carers for the congregation, and were responsible with the minister for the ordering of worship within the church. At first I found it rather difficult, having to remember always to consult the elders, but I learnt to welcome their support and input into what I was doing. The preparations for Sunday were undertaken by stewards (as in the Methodist pattern) and they were seen as the people responsible for the day to day running of the premises. The people took their responsibilities seriously and there never seemed to be a clash of interests.

A luncheon club for the estate was run by the people on a fortnightly basis, and meals on wheels taken out as part of this service. The people of the church were always open to new opportunities for outreach and the building was well used for all kinds of purposes. In my third year, in partnership with a local primary school, we founded an Out of School Club, for the many children in our surrounding area who had nowhere to go after school and, as I left, the church was seeking funding for the appointment of a detached youth worker to contact the many young people who hung around the estate and particularly around the premises at night. This particular work we saw as very important as there was a big problem on the estate with drink and drugs, and we had the largest proportion of single parent families in North Lincolnshire. As part of addressing this last question, the district nurse joined us in running parenting classes in the premises on a regular basis.

When I was appointed to go to Westcliff some people feared that such a role could not help but be a case of the 'lowest common denominator' in all areas of the church's life. I argued, and still would after my four years' experience, that it could equally well be seen as going for the 'highest common factor'.

*The Revd Pat Billsborrow*
*Methodist Minister*

❖ The **Bristol District** and the **Diocese of Bristol** are meeting to plan joint in-service training for local preachers and readers.

❖ In the **Diocese of Lincoln** and the **Lincoln and Grimsby District**, the Revd Elizabeth Smith, a Methodist minister, is serving her first appointment in the Church of England parish of New Clee.

❖ In Leeds, the **Leeds District** and the **Diocese of Ripon**, a deanery and a circuit, are exploring possibilities for growing together in ministry in an urban mission context.

❖ In the **York and Hull District**, and the **Diocese of York**, the District Probationer Secretary was a member of the Diocesan Board of Ministry.

❖ In Milton Keynes, in the **London North-West District** and the **Diocese of Oxford**, readers and local preachers are trained together, along with United Reformed Church and Baptist lay preachers.

❖ In Wolverhampton, the **Diocese of Lichfield** and the **Wolverhampton and Shrewsbury District**, the district ecumenical officer has found that he is increasingly invited to attend and address deanery synods and other Anglican meetings.

• How can you grow together in ministry in your area, sharing the work of ministers, readers and preachers?

• For Methodists, Recognized and Regarded or Authorized to Serve status is a useful resource, while Anglicans work within the provisions and permissions of Canon B 43 (for all Anglican churches) and B 44 (for Local Ecumenical Partnerships).

• How could you develop training and other resources for different kinds of ministry together?

# Growing Together in Social Responsibility and in Industrial Mission

❖ In the **Cornwall District** and the **Diocese of Truro**, the District Social Responsibility Committee has been disbanded, and the work is done through Church Social Responsibility in Cornwall, which is overseen by the Diocesan Council for Social Responsibility, and which works in partnership with the Roman Catholic and Russian Orthodox Churches.

## Case study: Hull Industrial Mission

In Hull the general work of the Industrial Mission team is an example of good practice. They work in a totally ecumenical way – the Board of Management has representatives from all the major denominations in the area, as well as people with no church connections. However, most of the funding comes from the Church of England and Methodist churches, and all the practical work is undertaken by Anglican and Methodist staff. Apart from the work done individually, the team programme includes regular events such as an Industrial Festival for the churches, regular lectures, and an annual Half Day Forum on a topic of current interest (in 1999 the subject was 'Regional Government and the Churches'). Apart from all this the Anglicans also appear on the preaching plans of both Methodist circuits and take services in local Methodist churches. They take this for granted as part of their common work.

Another example is more specific. It relates to a project recently set up called SEARCH (Social and Economic Action Resource of Churches in Hull). The purpose of this project is twofold. Firstly, to undertake an audit of churches in Hull to get a picture of the extent of their involvement in social action within their local communities. And, secondly, through this to stimulate them into developing their capacity to undertake further action, through providing advice and help about how to assess community needs, how to evaluate their existing capacity, and how to plan and implement new work, including accessing resources, training, volunteers, etc. So it is basically a capacity-building resource for local churches. This is a totally ecumenical project and aims to work with all churches in the area, and to bring groups of churches together to work on needs within their communities. It is being funded at the moment largely through the Church

Urban Fund and the Methodist Mission and Ministry Fund, with small contributions from local churches, the York Diocese and the Roman Catholic Middlesbrough Diocese.

But it all began with an initiative from the Anglican social responsibility officer, Methodist district social responsibility secretary, and Industrial Mission. They had jointly identified a need for information on what the churches were already doing and a concern about capacity to develop further work.

If you are involved in social responsibility or Industrial Mission –

- How could you work more effectively with your partner church?

- What are your partners already doing, which they could do on your behalf?

- Do you meet regularly to plan your work together and share ideas?

# Growing Together in Education

❖ The **London South-West District**, the **Eastbourne Circuit**, the **Diocese of Chichester** and the **Eastbourne Deanery** have signed an agreement to establish a new Anglican-Methodist primary school. The school, which will be known as the Haven School, is to be built in the rapidly growing area of Eastbourne around the new Sovereign Harbour. It is due to open in September 2001 and will accommodate 240 pupils, including 20 in a specialist speech and language learning difficulty unit. The school will house a Methodist-Anglican church and the school's diamond-shaped assembly hall has been designed to be suitable as a worship area. There are now 26 Church of England/Methodist schools in England, spread across 12 dioceses of the Church of England.

❖ In the **Diocese of Lincoln** and **Lincoln and Grimsby District**, a Methodist minister, serving in a Local Ecumenical Partnership, was a member of the Diocesan Board of Education.

❖ At the national level, the Further Education Adviser's post is jointly funded, half by the Methodists and half by the Church of England, and the Church of England's Youth Officer is a member of the Methodist Church Training Forum.

---

- How could you work together in all schools in your area?

- How are you and your partner church already involved in supporting all the phases of education: pre-school, primary and secondary schools, further education, higher education? How could you share this work?

- Do you share plans for new schools or projects with your partner churches?

- How could you work together to undertake more effective voluntary work with children and young people?

# Growing Together in the Structures of the Churches

❖ At the invitation of the **Cornwall District**, the Archdeacon of Cornwall represents the **Diocese of Truro** on the District Policy Committee, and the Bishop of Truro's Officer for Unity is a voting member of the District Property, Grants and Stationing Committee. The ecumenical officer and one other from the diocese are members of the district synod, who may speak but not vote; the ecumenical officer and one other from the district attend the diocesan synod as observers.

❖ In the **Diocese of Lincoln** and the **Lincoln and Grimsby District** there is reciprocal representation of district and diocesan synods, as well as on the United Reformed Church Provincial Synod.

❖ In the **Dioceses of Durham** and **Newcastle**, and the **Darlington** and **Newcastle-upon-Tyne Districts** there is reciprocal representation on synods which is no longer provided by the ecumenical officers, but by other significant people from the churches.

❖ In the **Diocese of Carlisle** and the **Cumbria District** the district ecumenical officer represents the district on the diocesan synod.

❖ In the **Diocese of Truro** and the **Cornwall District**, the Anglican Cathedral has made the Chairman of the District and the Roman Catholic Bishop of Plymouth Ecumenical Canons.

❖ In the **Diocese of York** and the **York and Hull District** the diocesan and district synods arranged their first joint meeting in April 2000. The diocesan secretary and district synod secretary have planned this together.

❖ In the **Diocese of Bradford** and the **West Yorkshire District** the district ecumenical officer is an observer on the diocesan synod, while in the **Diocese of Wakefield**, the same district ecumenical officer is a member of the Diocesan Ecumenical Affairs Committee.

- Do you have representatives from your partner church on your deanery, circuit, district or diocesan structures?

- How do you consult one another about important plans or decisions for the future?

- In your local church, how do you take counsel together?

# Growing Together in Oversight

❖ In the **North-East region**, the bishops and district chairmen meet for the day three times a year; their meetings include a balance of business, study and devotion and they find that eating together is an important dimension of their growth in friendship and the enjoyment of one another's company and support.

❖ The leaders of the Church of England and the Methodist Church, the Archbishops of Canterbury and York, the President and President-elect of Conference, meet annually for consultation and mutual encouragement.

❖ The House of Bishops and District Chairmen held their first joint meeting in January 2000.

● Amidst all the pressures and responsibilities which church leaders carry, how can they be encouraged to spend time together which has real value in terms of both personal support and the sharing of policy and resources?

# Growing Together During the Conversations

The beginning of the Formal Conversations has also stimulated many discussions specifically related to the conversations process, for example:

❖ The rural deans of the **Diocese of Blackburn** and the superintendent ministers of the **North Lancashire District** met at Whalley Abbey in September 1998 to begin discussion of the agenda for *Releasing Energy*: local discussion is now being encouraged.

❖ The rural deans of the East Riding in the **Diocese of York** and the superintendents of that area of the **York and Hull District** recently held a joint meeting.

❖ In 2000 the Church of England diocesan ecumenical officers and Methodist district ecumenical officers are sharing a joint annual consultation, rather than meeting separately.

## Case study: Durham

**Durham** has established a Local Conversations Group, which includes representatives of the diocese and of the Methodist **Newcastle** and **Darlington Districts**. The group includes the Methodist district chairmen, the Archdeacon of Durham, the ecumenical officers and other clergy and lay representatives of the two Churches. So far they have met three times and there has been an additional meeting between the three archdeacons of the diocese, the Methodist district chairmen and the diocesan ecumenical officer.

## Case study: Witney

BACKGROUND

Witney has a long history of Nonconformist Christian observance. John Wesley visited Witney on several occasions and the Methodist Society in Witney counted mill owners and workers among its number. The success of the Evangelical Revival led to Methodism becoming the major Nonconformist tradition in the area and opening a number of chapels in surrounding villages. The proliferation of Methodism in the eighteenth and nineteenth centuries meant that the Church of England did not hold the same dominant position in the town of Witney or in the surrounding villages during that period that it enjoyed in other parts of the country.

This legacy has been left to the Church of the twenty-first century. In the **Witney and Faringdon Circuit** a number of Methodist chapels in villages have closed but a good number remain. The point at which the comparison is most noticeable is in the town of Witney. There are two Methodist churches in the Ecclesiastical Parish of Witney with a combined membership of 372 (December 1997); the electoral roll of Witney Team Parish is 306 (January 1999). If one were to look at Churches in the Civic Parish of Witney the numbers would be different (3 Methodist churches, 385 members; 2 Anglican parishes, electoral roll 445) but the principle remains the same. The town of Witney has Anglican and Methodist churches of roughly equal strength and there is still a large number of outlying villages which have both Anglican and Methodist churches (the Anglican Deanery of Witney, which is entirely contained within the Witney and Faringdon Circuit, has 36 Anglican churches or centres of worship and 12 Methodist churches).

In the villages surrounding Witney both churches have small and ageing congregations. The agendas of the town and villages are different.

It is fair to say that there is a strong underlying conservatism in churches in this area. However, the population is expanding and becoming ever more mobile, and denominational labels are becoming less important within worshipping congregations.

It is also clear in the local area that there can be more significant differences of theology, liturgy and life within denominations than between them. The distinctive traditions and practices of the various churches are valued and contribute to the rich life of the whole church in the area, and the loss of such traditions is feared.

Within West Oxfordshire there are strong and weak congregations of both traditions. Talk of 'an Anglican-Methodist unity scheme' is always accompanied by talk of the fear of church closures. There is a particularly strong fear of closure among rural Methodist churches. This is coupled with a fear of a 'take-over' by the Church of England (possibly fuelled by there being many more Anglican than Methodist clergy). In Witney itself there is no such fear because of the historical and present-day strength of the Methodist societies.

There is a great deal of ecumenical cooperation and meeting in place at present. In Witney and the immediately surrounding villages nearly all of this takes place under the wider umbrella of Churches Together in Witney and District. In the villages outside the ambit of Churches Together in Witney ecumenical sharing is a more hit-and-miss affair. The success of joint worship in village churches is likewise patchy.

Various ecumenical projects have been undertaken, generally in the wider forum of Churches Together in Witney and District but occasionally in smaller units. In the centre of Witney Methodist, Congregational and Anglican churches have come together to employ a youth worker. In West Witney, Baptist, Methodist and Anglican churches cooperate in mission, outreach and children's work. These examples indicate the reality of an active ecumenism that extends further than our two denominations. Project-based work is a seemingly successful way to bring Christians of different traditions closer together. However, it has its weaknesses. One perceived problem with joint worship is that only a small percentage of worshippers worship ecumenically when given the chance; the same could be said of ecumenical projects. Moreover, even Christians who work together remain divided. In order for visible unity and the mutual accountability that would accompany it to be a reality, structural unity must be achieved.

Care needs to be taken not to damage the wider ecumenical relationships that each of our churches enjoys. This is true on a national level (thinking in particular of the relationship between the Methodist Church and the United Reformed Church) and also on a local level. However, it should be possible for local Anglican and Methodist churches to draw closer together without damaging relationships with other ecumenical partners.

## Suggestions to the churches

Against this background the Witney and Faringdon Methodist Circuit and the Witney Deanery (with the possible addition of neighbouring deaneries which fall within the area covered by the circuit) are considering the following suggestions:

- the sharing of worship in places where both denominations are represented and where shared worship does not generally take place;

- encouragement to each denomination to pray for the other and for those taking part in Formal Conversations;

- the invitation of lay and ordained ministers of each denomination to take part in the leading of worship in the other (regulations for ministers of other churches to function within the Church of England are set out in Canon B 43);

- joint meetings of circuit ministers and deanery chapters;

- an examination of where ministry is duplicated, e.g. in the field of social responsibility;

- an examination of the needs of the rural church and how the ministry of both churches could be more effectively deployed;

- constructive use of the *Declaration of Ecumenical Welcome* in places where there is only one church in a particular settlement;

- a sharing of resources for the training of local preachers and licensed lay ministers (formerly readers).

The concern of this discussion has been to see how the prospect of Anglican/Methodist unity would be received in the local church. Some hard work is needed to dispel the myth and mutual suspicion that has built up over 200 years of separation. Sensitivity is needed in listening to the concerns and worries of those who are sceptical of the proposals.

*Revd Will Adam*
*Anglican priest*

- During the conversations, how can you and your partner church take these suggestions forward?

# Declarations of Ecumenical Welcome and Commitment:

Resources for taking this work forward locally

# WHEN THE ANGLICAN CHURCH IS THE ONLY CHURCH IN A VILLAGE

## Suggestions and guidelines

1.      In many villages there is only one church building and worshipping community, most often Church of England. Within the village there may be Christians of different traditions, some of whom try to combine loyalty to a particular denomination with their desire to worship and witness in their local community. Sometimes a church of another denomination has been closed, sometimes people from another denomination have moved into the village, sometimes those who previously commuted to a church outside the village are prevented from doing so through infirmity or poor public transport.

2.      The aim of parochial church councils and incumbents will be to make members of other denominations feel at home in their local Anglican church, and to feel that they belong to the Christian community in that place. The sense of belonging and being valued may not for everyone be the same as 'being a member'. This is because not all those of other denominations are able, because of their denomination's rules, to declare themselves also to be members of the Church of England (as the Church of Representation Rules permit).

3.      The church making this declaration, whilst remaining subject to the jurisdiction of the Church of England and guardian of its tradition, formulates a policy towards those of other denominations which enables their insights, strengths, gifts and graces to be incorporated into the whole life of the congregation. That life will include worship, mission and service, as well as the administrative and decision-making processes.

4.      There may be occasions when those of another denomination worshipping in the parish church wish to express their membership and belonging in a particular way, for example when the tradition with which they have been familiar has a membership structure more closely defined than that of the Church of England. This could be expressed through a short welcome, prayer, and the right hand of fellowship which could take place at the Peace.

5.     The congregation of the parish church will want to be especially aware of its responsibility to be broad, flexible and open, and to affirm a diversity of religious experience and expression. (This applies to the variety of emphases within a denomination, as well as between the various denominational traditions.) Breadth and openness could be affirmed through:

- choice of hymns, tunes and hymn-books;

- prayers for other churches and their leaders;

- invitations to ministers of other traditions to participate in leading worship or preaching (as allowed by Canon B 43);

- occasional use of other denominations' liturgies (as allowed by Canon B 43);

- occasional use of other practices of administering Holy Communion;

- careful use of language which includes and is not specific to one denomination;

- offering occasional (or regular) use of church buildings to other Christian traditions;

- use of non-eucharistic services to bridge the divide of eucharistic hospitality between Roman Catholics and other churches;

- consultation between those with pastoral oversight in the area about the responsibility of care, initiation, nurture, etc.

6.     Before a single church agrees a *Declaration of Ecumenical Welcome and Commitment* it should seek advice from the 'intermediate body' or its ecumenical officer as to which other denominations should be consulted, and at what level. The Group for Local Unity of Churches together in England suggests that for the Methodist Church this should be the circuit superintendent and stewards, and for the United Reformed Church, the church secretary and the President of the District Council. Care needs to be taken over the real or imagined effect on the congregational strength of these churches, so that this is not seen as 'poaching'. Sensitivity is needed to the existence of small groups of Christians, who may be meeting for worship in local houses in some situations, so that this initiative is not perceived as Anglican imperialism. A copy of the *Declaration* should be displayed in the church.

# A Declaration of Ecumenical Welcome and Commitment

## By a Church of England parish

1.      We, the *Vicar* and people of St CCC's, are aware that St CCC's is the only church in *Aford*, and therefore we invite all Christians in *Aford* to be as fully a part of our life and fellowship as they are able.

2.      We invite those of Christian traditions other than our own:

- to share in the ministry and mission of the Church in this community;

- to worship and, if baptized and communicant members of other churches, to receive Holy Communion at St CCC's;

- to be part of the decision-making of the church and to contribute to a common fund for the mission and ministry of the wider Church in so far as their continued giving to another church will allow.[2]

3.      We undertake:

- to give pastoral care to all those who desire it;

- to invite ministers of other churches to take part in leading worship;[3]

- to incorporate the riches of worship of other traditions as appropriate;[4]

- to consult with neighbouring churches concerning the mission of the church in *Aford*;

- to include this ecumenical declaration as an integral part of the parish profile.

4.      Following the decision made by Churches Together in *Ashire* (our 'intermediate body') on . . . . . . . . . . . . . . . . . . 200X that such declarations may be made in the area which they serve, we have sought and followed their advice as to which churches should first be consulted, and those mentioned below have given us their blessing and encouragement.

**for St CCC's Aford Vicar**_____

**Church Wardens**          _____

**for other churches: signature** _____

**on behalf of**  _____

## Declarations of Ecumenical Welcome and Commitment

[1] Canon B 15a (1972) enables the admission to Holy Communion of 'baptized persons who are communicant members of other churches which subscribe to the doctrine of the Holy Trinity, and who are in good standing in their own church . . .' If anyone by virtue of this provision 'regularly receives the Holy Communion over a long period which appears likely to continue indefinitely, the minister shall set before him the normal requirements of the Church of England for communicant status of that Church.'

[2] The Church Representation Rules 1995 enable a person to be enrolled if she/he is baptized, sixteen years or upwards and declares themselves 'to be a member in good standing of a Church which subscribes to the doctrine of the Holy Trinity . . . and also prepared to declare himself to be a member of the Church of England having habitually attended public worship in the parish during a period of six months prior to enrolment.' Making this declaration also confers eligibility to stand for election to the decision-making bodies of the Church of England.

[3] Canon B 43 (1989) says:

*A minister or lay person who is a member in good standing of a church to which this Canon applies and is a baptized person may, subject to the provisions of this Canon, be invited to perform all or any of the following duties —*

(a) *to say or sing Morning or Evening Prayer;*

(b) *to read the Holy Scripture at any service;*

(c) *to preach at any service;*

(d) *to lead the intercessions at the Holy Communion and to lead prayers at other services;*

(e) *to assist at baptism or the solemnization of matrimony or conduct a funeral service;*

(f) *to assist in the distribution of the holy sacrament of the Lord's Supper to the people at the Holy Communion if the minister or lay person is authorized to perform a similar duty in his or her own church.*

[4] Canon B 43 (1989) says:

*9. The incumbent of a parish may (with specified approval) invite members of another church . . . to take part in joint worship with the Church of England or to use a church in the parish for worship in accordance with the forms of service and practice of that other church on such occasions as may be specified in the approval given by the bishop.*

# When the Methodist church is the only church in a village

## Suggestions and guidelines

1.      In many villages there is only one church building and worshipping community. In some villages this will be a Methodist church. Within the village there may be Christians of different traditions, some of whom try to combine loyalty to a particular denomination with their desire to worship and witness in their local community. Sometimes a church of another denomination has been closed, sometimes people from another denomination have moved into the village, sometimes those who previously commuted to a church outside the village are prevented from doing so through infirmity or poor public transport.

2.      While the local church will belong within a circuit and be part of the wider Methodist connexion, it is able in a variety of ways to make members of other churches feel that they belong to the Christian community in that village. This sense of belonging may not be the same as becoming a member of that local church. Some churches do not permit their members to become members of another church and some individuals may feel that their sense of denominational identity is such that they are unable or unwilling to become members of the Methodist Church.

They may, however, be willing to be on the community roll of the church and take as full a part as possible in its worship and life.

3.      The local church will want to welcome all who wish to be part of its fellowship and enable their insights, strengths, gifts and graces to be incorporated into the whole life of the congregation. That life will include worship, mission and service, as well as the administrative and decision-making process.

4.      The minister and congregation of the Methodist church will want to be especially aware of their responsibility to be broad, flexible and open, and to affirm a diversity of religious experience and expression. Breadth and openness could be affirmed through:

- choice of hymns, tunes and hymn-books;
- prayers for other churches and their leaders;

- invitations to ministers/preachers/readers of other traditions to lead worship;

- occasional use of other denominations' liturgies and ways of administering Holy Communion;

- careful use of language which includes and is not specific to one denomination;

- offering use of church buildings to other Christian traditions;

- consultation between those with pastoral oversight in the area about matters of mutual concern and responsibility;

- involvement in the life of the wider church through Churches Together groupings.

5.      The local church may wish to formalize and ensure the continuity of this ecumenically enriched life by agreeing a *Declaration of Ecumenical Welcome*. Before doing so it should seek advice from the intermediate body or the district ecumenical officer as to which other denominations should be consulted, and at what level. The *Declaration* must be endorsed by the neighbouring churches and care needs to be taken over the real or imagined effect on the congregational strength of these churches so that this is not seen as 'poaching'. A copy of the *Declaration* should be displayed in the church.

# A Declaration of Ecumenical Welcome And Commitment

## By a Methodist Church

1. We, the minister and members of *Aford* Methodist Church, are aware we are the only church in *Aford*, and therefore we invite all Christians in *Aford* to be as fully a part of our life and fellowship as they are able.

2. We invite those of Christian traditions other than our own:

- to share in the ministry and mission of the Church in this community;

- to worship and, if baptized and communicant members of other Churches, to receive Holy Communion with us;

- to share in the decision-making and leadership of the church[1] and to contribute financially to *Aford* Methodist Church in so far as their continued giving to another church will allow.

3. We undertake:

- to give pastoral care to all those who desire it;

- to incorporate the riches of worship of other traditions as appropriate;

- to invite ministers and lay preachers of other churches to take part in leading worship;

- to consult with neighbouring churches concerning the mission of the church in *Aford*.

4. Following the decision made by Churches Together in *Ashire* (our 'intermediate body') on . . . . . . . . . . . . . . . . . . . 200X that such declarations may be made in the area which they serve, we have sought and followed their advice as to which churches should first be consulted, and those mentioned below have given us their blessing and encouragement.

**for Aford Methodist Church Minister** _____

**Church Stewards** _____

**for other churches: signature** _____

**on behalf of** _____

[1] Standing Order 610(3) says:

'The Church Council may invite other members of the Local Church and non-members who are active in the life of the church to attend meetings of the Church Council and shall in particular, wherever possible, encourage young people to do so. Those who thus attend are not members of the council; they are entitled to speak but not to vote nor to propose or second any resolution.

# Sources of Information and Advice for Taking This Work Forward Together

## In the Methodist Church

Each district has an ecumenical officer, from whom advice and information can be obtained.

The Coordinating Secretary responsible for this area of work who is also the ecumenical officer for the Methodist Church is **Revd Peter Sulston, Methodist Church House, 25 Marylebone Road, London NW1 5JR. Tel: 020 7486 5502; Fax 020 7467 5228; email: co-ordsec@methodistchurch.org.uk**

The secretary of the Methodist Committee for Local Ecumenical Development is **Deacon Jane Middleton, at The Rectory, 35 Dane Road, Warlingham, Surrey, CR6 9NP.**

## In the Church of England

Each diocese has a diocesan ecumenical officer who will be able to offer support and encouragement for churches who want to take up the questions and challenges of this book and information about the Ecumenical Canons B 43 and B 44. Your diocesan ecumenical officer can be contacted through the diocesan office.

Also available to offer any additional advice are the staff of the Council for Christian Unity, based at Church House, Westminster, in particular **Revd Flora Winfield, Secretary for Local Unity, The Council for Christian Unity, Church House, Great Smith Street, London SW1P 3NZ. Tel: 020 7898 1471; Fax: 020 7898 1483; email: flora.winfield@ccu.c-of-e.org.uk**

- If you want to respond to the material in this book or have local experience that you would like to share, please contact either Revd Peter Sulston or Revd Flora Winfield at the addresses given above.

The heart of ecumenism is renewal . . . we need to dwell far less upon our ecclesiastical structures and far more upon what we can do together as Christians, learning from one another across the denominational borders, in the deepening of spirituality, in the exploring of theological depth, in evangelism together and in together saying something and doing something towards the secular community beyond the Church's frontier.

**Archbishop Michael Ramsey**
**to the General Synod**
**May 1972**